Packing up a Picnic

Activities and Recipes for Kids

Rick Walton & Jennifer Adams
Illustrated by Debra Spina Dixon

Gibbs Smith, Publisher
Salt Lake City

First Edition

10 09 08 07 06   5 4 3 2 1

Text © 2006 Rick Walton and Jennifer Adams

Illustrations © 2006 Debra Dixon

Published by

Gibbs Smith, Publisher

P.O. Box 667

Layton, Utah 84041

Orders: 1.800.748.5439

www.gibbs-smith.com

Designed by Dawn DeVries Sokol

Printed and bound in Hong Kong

Library of Congress Cataloging-in-Publication Data

Walton, Rick.

   Packing up a picnic : activities and recipes for kids / Rick Walton and

Jennifer Adams.— 1st ed.

         p. cm.

   ISBN 1-58685-778-9

   1. Picnicking—Juvenile literature.   I. Adams, Jennifer. II. Title.

TX823.W284 2006

641.5'78—dc22

To Ann, Alan, Patrick, Nicholas, Sarah and David,
my favorite picnic partners—RW

To my dad, for packing up many picnics—JA

Contents

Let's Picnic! 6

Breakfast Picnic 10

Bicycle Picnic...16

Haunted Picnic 22

Snow Picnic 30

Surprise Picnic 40

Beach Picnic 46

Drive-in Picnic...54

Create Your Own Picnic 62

Let's Picnic!

Summer is a wonderful time for picnics. So is spring, fall, and winter. Grab your favorite foods, head to a park, spread out a blanket, and chow down. Somehow food seems to taste better when it's eaten outside.

But not every picnic needs to be eaten in a park, and not every picnic basket needs to contain fried chicken and potato salad. Picnicking is a chance to use your imagination and have fun.

In this book you will find seven fun, creative, unusual picnics for kids of all ages. There are also a lot of easy recipes for yummy food—the star of any picnic.

A **PICNIC** used to be a meal where everyone brought some food. It didn't become an outdoor event until the nineteenth century.

WHAT YOU WILL NEED FOR YOUR PICNIC

Each picnic you plan will be different, but you should always take the following:

◆ Something to hold your picnic—a picnic basket, bag, box, cooler, or something else that will easily hold your food.

◆ Something to put your picnic on—a blanket, sheet, or tablecloth.

- ◆ Something to eat your picnic with—paper plates, paper cups, plasticware, and napkins.

- ◆ Things to keep you safe and healthy—sunscreen, insect repellent, and hand sanitizer.

- ◆ Something to clean up with—moist towelettes, paper towels, and a small sack for garbage if there are no garbage cans nearby.

Don't Get Sick!

Germs love food that's been left out too long. The best way to keep them from eating your picnic before you do is to always wash your hands before and after handling food. This will chase away germs.

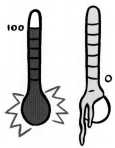

Keep your cold foods cold and your hot foods hot. Cold foods should be eaten within four hours, and hot foods within two hours of them coming to room temperature.

Cold leftovers can be taken home if they are kept cold, but any hot leftovers should be thrown away.

Keep It Cool (or Warm)

To keep cold food cold, put it in an insulated container (a cooler, an insulated backpack, or a lunchbox).

Put something in to keep it cold (ice, gel packs, or frozen juice boxes).

To keep warm foods warm, put them in an insulated container WITHOUT anything cold. The heat from the food will keep the food warm.

Choosing a Spot

Your picnic spot should allow you to have lots of fun with no problems.

Some things you might want at your picnic spot:

- grass
- shade
- room to run
- fun things to do
- restrooms
- water fountains

Some things you don't want at your picnic spot:

- traffic
- garbage
- too much noise
- dangerous things going on
- anthills or beehives
- mosquitoes
- an angry person who doesn't want you on their property

Watch the **weather.** Have a backup picnic place in mind in case of rain, wind, or snow.

Breakfast Picnic

Wake before dawn to enjoy a breakfast picnic while watching the sun rise. Hold your picnic on your front lawn, in a park, on a mountain overlook, or even on top of a building—any place that gives you a view of the rising sun.

PICNIC FOOD

◆ Sunrise Breakfast Sandwich
◆ **Toothpick Fruit Dippers and Yogurt**
◆ Orange Juice

SUNRISE BREAKFAST SANDWICH

What you need:

◆ 1 egg
◆ 2 slices of bread
◆ butter
◆ 2 slices of ham
◆ 1 slice of cheese

What you do:

1. Crack the egg in a nonstick frying pan and cook over medium heat until it is well done. You don't want the center to be runny.

2. Toast the bread and butter it.

3. Put together your sandwich by placing the fried egg on the buttered side of one piece of toast. Top with slices of ham and cheese. Put the other piece of toast on top with the buttered side facing the cheese.

Makes 1 sandwich

TOOTHPICK FRUIT DIPPERS AND YOGURT

What you need:

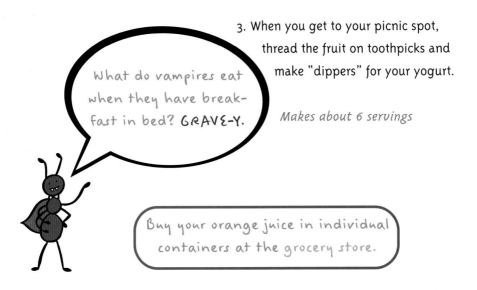

- 2 cups strawberries, blueberries, pineapple chunks, apple slices, and/or grapes
- Toothpicks
- Yogurt, any flavor

What you do:

1. Wash the berries and grapes and wash and slice the apples.

2. Put the fruit in plastic zippered bags.

3. When you get to your picnic spot, thread the fruit on toothpicks and make "dippers" for your yogurt.

Makes about 6 servings

What do vampires eat when they have break-fast in bed? GRAVE-Y.

Buy your orange juice in individual containers at the grocery store.

PICNIC FUN

SUNRISE CONTEST
What you need:

- paper
- pen or pencil
- a watch

What you do:

As soon as you arrive at your viewing spot, have everyone guess the exact time (hour and minutes) that the sun will appear over the horizon. Write down the guesses.

Assign one person to keep track of the time. Play other games until the sun is about to appear. Then sit in silence and watch.

The moment that any part of the sun appears, everyone cheer loudly. After the sun first starts to appear, it is not a good idea to keep watching it. Staring directly at the sun can damage your eyes.

The timekeeper announces the exact time of sunrise. Look at your paper to see who guessed the closest. The winner gets to choose what the group does next.

When do ducks wake up in the morning? **AT THE QUACK OF DAWN.**

WHAT DO YOU HEAR?

What you do:

Sit quietly and count all the different types of sounds you hear—birds, the wind, cars, planes, the rustle of branches, breathing, the bark of a dog.

When you hear a sound, quietly describe what you hear. Count how many different things the group hears.

I Spy

What you do:

Choose one player to be the Spy.

The Spy looks around, selects something, and then says, "I spy with my little eye something that is . . . " Then the Spy gives an adjective that describes that thing, for example, "something green," "something big," or "something round."

Other players try to guess what the Spy is seeing. If they cannot guess the object, the Spy gives them another clue. The player who guesses right is the next Spy.

BALLOON RACE

What you need:

◆ Party balloons
◆ An open place to play

What you do:

Blow up the balloons, tie them shut, and give one to each person. Pick a starting line and a finish line. Everyone places his or her balloon on the starting line and stands behind it.

One person is chosen to start the race. When she says "GO!" the players start kicking or bumping their balloons forward. You can use any part of your body except for your hands and arms.

The first one to get his or her balloon over the finish line wins.

> Make sure you play this game somewhere safe, where you won't fall and hurt yourself.

Bicycle Picnic

Why does a picnic have to be held in just one spot? Why not a traveling picnic—ride a little, eat a little, ride a little, eat a little. It's fun to work up an appetite and then stop to satisfy it.

REMEMBER:

Bike riding is a lot of fun, but it can be dangerous if you are not careful. Be sure to obey all bike safety rules. Wear a helmet, watch for traffic, don't ride too fast, and be safe. You don't want your picnic lunch to end up being hospital food!

PICNIC FOOD

◆ Italian Club Rollups
◆ Spokes and Wheels Trail Mix
◆ Oranges or Mandarin Orange Fruit Cups

ITALIAN CLUB ROLLUPS

What you need:

◆ 1 flour tortilla
◆ 2 slices of ham
◆ 2 slices of salami
◆ 2 slices of Swiss or provolone cheese

◆ 1 teaspoon olive oil
◆ 1/4 teaspoon dry oregano
◆ toothpicks

What you do:

1. Lay the tortilla flat on a work space.

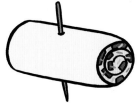

2. Place ham on top, overlapping the ham as little as possible while covering the whole tortilla.

3. Cover ham with the salami, and then top with cheese.

4. Drizzle with olive oil, and then sprinkle with oregano.

5. Starting on one side, roll up the sandwich like a burrito. Cut it in half and secure with toothpicks.

6. Place in zippered plastic sandwich bags to carry to your picnic.

Makes 2 rollups

SPOKES AND WHEELS TRAIL MIX

What you need:

- ◆ 1 cup pretzel rods
- ◆ 1 cup dried banana chips
- ◆ 1 cup raisins
- ◆ 1 cup peanuts or almonds
- ◆ 1 cup M&Ms

What you do:

1. Mix all the ingredients together in a big bowl.

2. Separate evenly into 10 zippered plastic bags.

Makes 5 trail mix snacks

Buy fresh oranges or individual mandarin orange fruit cups at the grocery store.

PICNIC FUN

RED LIGHT, GREEN LIGHT

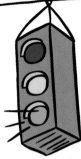

What you do:

Pick a place where you won't be near traffic. Choose one person to be "It."

Choose a starting line and a finish line. "It" sits on his bike at the finish line. Everyone else sits on their bikes at the starting line. They face each other.

"It" shouts "Green Light!" and turns around, then counts loudly and quickly to ten. He then turns back and shouts, "Red Light!"

After "It" shouts "Green Light!" the rest of the players ride their bikes toward the finish line, stopping before "It" shouts, "Red Light!"

If "It" can catch anyone's bike still moving forward, he calls out their name and they have to go back to the starting line. The first player to cross the finish line wins and is the next "It."

What's the difference between a bicycle tire and a haunted house? ONE IS FULL OF SPOKES, THE OTHER IS FULL OF SPOOKS.

Scavenger Hunts

What you need:

- A backpack or a bag each player can fasten to their bike to put things into.
- A list of things to look for.

Here is a list to get you started on your first hunt. You can make up your own lists too.

flower
stick
red rock
flyer
leaf
coin

What you do:

As you ride along, watch for the things on your list. When you see one, stop and put it in your bag. The first person to find everything on the list wins.

Another way to play is to have a **visual scavenger hunt.** Instead of picking things up, just look for things, like a rose bush, a tricycle, someone walking a dog, or a police car.

Help out your community by making your hunt a litter hunt. Your list might include such things as an empty pop can, a gum wrapper, a candy bar wrapper, a newspaper, a box, or an old shoe.

I'd rather be an ant than a litter bug.

SALE!

See who can find the weirdest piece of garbage. Be careful not to pick up anything that looks sharp or dangerous. Use a plastic or paper sack to put the litter in, and then throw the sacks away in a big garbage can.

LOOK OUT! When you are hunting, the most important thing is to stay safe. Watch the road ahead of you at all times. Don't ride fast while you are searching. Never pick up anything that looks dangerous or disgusting.

ENJOYING THE RIDE

Sometimes the best thing to do on a bike ride is nothing. Just ride along, enjoying the speed, the wind in your face, the sites and the sounds. Stop where you want to stop, play where you want to play, eat where you want to eat, and ride where you want to ride.

Haunted Picnic

A dark night, eerie noises just past the shadows, stories of monsters—this picnic is guaranteed to make you shiver with delight!

Hold your picnic in a fort, tree house, tent, clubhouse, or out in the open under the dark starry sky. There's nothing like a haunted picnic during a sleepover.

PICNIC FOOD

◆ Seven Layer Dip with Chips
◆ **Bag of Eyeballs**
◆ Ghost-in-the-Graveyard Cupcakes

SEVEN LAYER DIP

What you need:

◆ 1 (15-ounce) can refried beans
◆ 1 cup sour cream
◆ 1 cup salsa
◆ ½ cup grated cheddar cheese
◆ ½ cup grated Monterey Jack cheese
◆ sliced olives
◆ sliced green onions
◆ tortilla chips

Who did the ghost take with him on his picnic? HIS GHOUL FRIEND.

What you do:

1. Get 2 individual plastic food storage keepers or other small containers with lids. Spread half the beans in the bottom of each one.

2. Spread half the sour cream over the beans in each container.

3. Pour half the salsa over the top of each, then sprinkle half the cheese on top of each.

4. Top each with sliced olives and green onions.

5. Dip the tortilla chips into the bean dip and enjoy.

Makes 4 servings

BAG OF EYEBALLS

What you need:

◆ 1 big bunch of red grapes

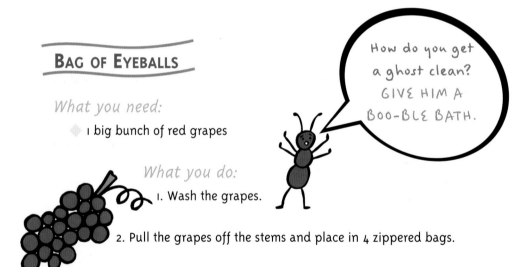

How do you get a ghost clean? GIVE HIM A BOO-BLE BATH.

What you do:

1. Wash the grapes.

2. Pull the grapes off the stems and place in 4 zippered bags.

If you want your bag of eyeballs to feel really creepy, or for a nighttime picnic, carefully peel the grapes before putting them in the bag. Throw the peelings away.

Makes 4 servings

24

Ghost-in-the-Graveyard Cupcakes

What you need:

- ◆ 1 white or devil's food cake mix
- ◆ 1 can of chocolate frosting
- ◆ 24 Nutter-Butter cookies
- ◆ 1 can of vanilla frosting
- ◆ 1 tube of chocolate decorator's icing

What you do:

1. Make the cupcakes according to the package directions. Use cupcake liners.

2. When the cupcakes are cool, frost each one with chocolate frosting.

3. Stick a Nutter-Butter cookie part way into the top of each frosted cupcake so it stands up.

4. Frost the part of the cookie that is sticking out of the top with vanilla frosting.

5. Draw eyes and a mouth on your ghost with the chocolate decorator's icing.

Makes 24 cupcakes

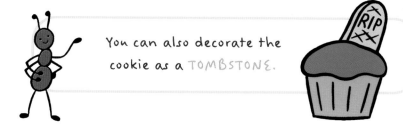

You can also decorate the cookie as a TOMBSTONE.

PICNIC FUN

SOME OF THESE GAMES CAN BE PRETTY SCARY. If you have young kids (or easily scared older kids or grownups) on this picnic, you might want to tone down some of the fright. Turn on a light. Stay close to the house. Make your stories about something safer— like an angry bunny.

But if you're all brave kids who like chills and shivers, scare away!

*It's more fun to play these games **without** flashlights!*

GHOST IN THE GRAVEYARD

3 or more players

Decide the following:

The Hiding Area—Players can't go outside this area. It could be just your yard, your yard and the neighbor's yard, or your yard and the haunted forest beyond.

RIP

The Ghost—One of you. You don't have to be a real ghost, but if one of you is a real ghost, all the better.

Home Base—This can be a tree, a porch, a bench, a coffin . . . it's the spot where everyone is safe from the Ghost (but not necessarily goblins, vampires, and werewolves. They're not supposed to play this game, but you try telling that to them!)

What you do:

Everyone but the Ghost stands at home base, closes their eyes, and counts slowly to midnight (one o'clock, two o'clock, three o'clock . . . all the way up to MIDNIGHT—that's twelve o'clock). While they count, the Ghost hides.

At midnight, everyone opens their eyes and sets out into the dark to look for the

Ghost. You can chant, "No ghosts are out tonight!" or you can merely cringe and whimper in fear. The first person to see the hidden Ghost shouts, **"GHOST IN THE GRAVE-YARD!"** and everyone races back to home base. If the Ghost tags any players before they reach home base, they are now Ghosts too.

All Ghosts now hide while the rest of the players count. The last person to become a Ghost is the first Ghost for the next round.

Murder in the Dark

3 or more players

What you need:

Get a white strip of paper for each player. On one strip write an X. Fold the strips and put them in a bag or bowl.

What you do:

Everyone sits in a circle and carefully draws out a strip of paper without showing each other what's on it. The person with the X strip is "It."

Hold hands. "It" starts killing by squeezing the hand of someone next to him. To kill someone two people away, for example, "It" would squeeze two times.

The person who receives squeezes will then squeeze the next person's hand that many times minus one. For example, if you get two squeezes, you give one squeeze to the next person.

If you receive one squeeze—you're dead! Let go of hands and die dramatically. The remaining players join hands and continue.

If you think you know who the murderer is, let go of hands quickly, and ACCUSE! If you're right, you win. If you're wrong . . . you're dead.

When the murderer is discovered, or everyone is dead, start over.

Spooky Stories

Take turns making up spooky stories. Tell them in a serious voice, perhaps with a flash-light shining up toward your face, giving you the look of a disembodied head.

Your story should have:

A scary creature—a ghost, vampire, werewolf, mutant, giant bug, killer gorilla—something scary that might be lurking out there in the shadows.

A victim or victims, someone the scary creature is after, like someone in your group.

A place where your story is set. Someplace you've all been, or maybe—right here.

A time when your story takes place—like right now.

Build the suspense. Have the scary creature come slowly . . . slowly. Have your victims be more and more frightened.

During your story, make it clear that the creature might be out there right now, as you speak. In fact, over there, in the shadows—could it be?

Have your creature ATTACK! Shout, and grab the person next to you. Then laugh yourself silly as everyone shouts and screams in fear.

Snow Picnic

There's nothing like hot food on a cold day. Dive into the snow—run in it, roll in it, play in it—and then warm up with warm food and wassail. Who says picnics are only for summer?

PICNIC FOOD

◆ **Baked Chicken**
◆ Easy Potato Salad
◆ **Ants on a Log**
◆ Wassail

BAKED CHICKEN

What you need:

◆ 4 chicken drumsticks

◆ ½ stick butter or margarine

◆ 2 cups cornflakes

◆ ½ cup Parmesan cheese

What you do:

1. Preheat the oven to 350 degrees.

2. Rinse the chicken and pat dry with paper towels. Put them on a clean plate.

3. Melt the butter in the microwave in a microwave-safe bowl.

What do chickens grow on?
EGGPLANTS!

4. Put the cornflakes in a quart-size zippered plastic bag. Push out the extra air and then seal the bag. Crush the cornflakes in the bag with a rolling pin.

5. Open the bag and add the cheese. Carefully reseal the bag shut, and then shake it to mix the cornflakes and cheese. Pour the crushed mixture into an empty pie pan.

6. Dip the chicken in the butter, and then roll it in the cornflakes.

7. Put chicken on a cookie sheet and bake for 30 minutes. You or an adult can test to see if it is done by carefully cutting into it once it is removed from the oven. If it's not pink inside anymore, then it's finished.

Makes 4 servings

EASY POTATO SALAD

What you need:

- ◆ 6 red potatoes
- ◆ 1 cup bottled ranch dressing

When you make potato salad, you need to cook the potatoes ahead of time (at least an hour or two) so they have time to cool.

What you do:

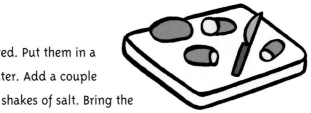

1. Peel the potatoes, if desired. Put them in a pot and cover with cold water. Add a couple shakes of salt. Bring the water in the pan to a boil.

2. Let the potatoes boil for 20 minutes or until you can stick them with a fork and it goes in easily. Have an adult help you test to see if they are done and be careful not to get burned.

3. When the potatoes are done, drain off the water and put them in a bowl. Cover with plastic wrap and put them in the refrigerator to cool down.

4. When they are cool, cut them into cubes and put them in a large bowl.

5. Add the ranch dressing and mix well.

Makes 4 to 6 servings

Remember, **potato salad** has to be kept in the refrigerator or in a cooler with ice until you eat it.

ANTS ON A LOG

What you need:
- ◆ 2 celery sticks
- ◆ peanut butter
- ◆ raisins

What you do:

1. Wash the celery. Cut off the ends, and then cut each stalk in half across the width. You will have 4 pieces. Do this before you leave for your picnic. Do the rest of the steps after you get to your picnic spot.

2. With a butter knife, spread peanut butter inside the celery sticks.

3. Press a line of raisins gently into the peanut butter.

Makes 2 servings (2 each)

What do you get when you cross some ants with some ticks?
ALL SORTS OF ANTICS!

WASSAIL

What you need:

- 6 cups apple cider or apple juice
- 2 cups orange juice
- 2 cinnamon sticks
- 2 lemon slices

What you do:

1. Combine all the ingredients in a pot. Heat over medium heat until warmed through.

2. Use a slotted spoon to take out the lemon slices and cinnamon sticks. Throw them away.

3. Put the wassail in a thermos to keep it warm. Serve the wassail in mugs or foam cups.

Makes 8 servings

PICNIC FUN

BUILD A SNOWMAN

What you need:

- ◆ Lots of good packing snow
- ◆ Warm clothes, especially gloves
- ◆ Fun stuff to decorate your snowman with, like rocks, buttons, sticks, carrots, potatoes, yarn, a hat and scarf, or other creative objects

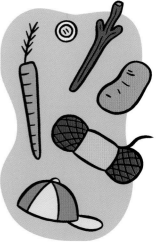

What you do:

Basic snowman—

Roll three balls of snow: a large ball for the base, a medium-size ball for the torso, and a smaller ball for the head. Stack them up.

Push sticks or branches into the torso to give the snowman arms.

Hint: If the snowballs keep falling off, push a stick halfway into the bottom ball and push the top ball down onto the stick's other half.

Give the snowman a face and dress him in a hat and scarf.

Advanced snowman—
Don't just leave your snowman standing—pose him. Build him waving, sleeping, kneeling, covering his eyes, screaming in horror, or pointing.

Give your snowman interesting expressions—make him happy, sad, laughing, confused, astonished, angry, or terrified. Give him an upside-down face or a mustache. Put eyes in the back of his head. Have fun with him.

Why a snow *man*? Make a snow woman. A snow baby. A snow family. A snow dog. A snow dragon.

Mix three drops of food coloring with water in a spray bottle. Spray it on your snowman, and he will become multicolored in no time.

Snow Sculpture Contest

See who can build the most interesting snow sculpture.

Some tips and tricks:

Use a snow shovel to build a mound of snow to start carving.

Use bowls, glasses, and other containers to create interesting shapes for your sculpture.

Use spatulas, spoons, and other kitchen devices as carving tools.

If the snow is too dry to stick together, fill a spray bottle with water and spray the snow.

Mix three drops of food coloring with water in a spray bottle. Spray color on your sculpture to create a work of art.

SNOWLYMPICS

See who's the coolest athlete in town. Have fun playing these snow games.

Long jump—Use your foot or a stick to draw a starting line in the snow. Take turns running up to the line and jumping as far as you can.

Hurdles—Define a course in the snow that you will run. Don't pack down the snow. If the snow is deep and soft it will be more fun. Every 10 or 20 feet build a short wall, like a hurdle, out of loosely packed snow. Race along the course and try to jump over the hurdles without hitting them.

High jump—Build a wall about 2 feet high out of snow. Take turns jumping over it. After everyone has jumped, pile on another few inches of snow. Everyone who made it over without touching the wall jumps again. Repeat until the wall is too high for anyone to jump over. The person who jumps the highest wall wins.

Shot put—Each athlete builds a snowball as big as his or her head. Take turns seeing who can throw their snowball the farthest.

SNOW ANGELS

What you need:
A clean, untouched area of snow.

What you do:
Carefully fall backwards into the snow. With your arms out straight, move them from your waist to above your head, brushing the snow aside to make the angel wings.

With your legs out straight, move them apart and together several times, brushing the snow away to make the angel's robe.

Have a friend stand at your feet, grab your hands, and help you up. Try not to step on your angel. See if you can invent other shapes in the snow.

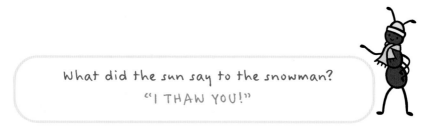

What did the sun say to the snowman?
"I THAW YOU!"

Surprise Picnic

Do you like surprises? Do you like new experiences? Then this picnic is for you.

With a surprise location and menu, this kind of picnic will never be boring.

You'll have to guess what's going to happen next.

What you do:

Pick a location—Pass out strips of paper to each person going on the picnic. Have each person write a location on the strip, fold it, and put it in a bag.

Wherever you go, make sure you take a garbage sack to carry out your trash.

Have the youngest person pick a strip out of the bag. The location written on the strip is where you will have your picnic.

Pick the food—Everyone goes together to a grocery store. Split up. Each person chooses one or two ready-to-eat foods. Whatever people choose is what the group eats for the picnic.

You'll probably get some interesting combinations, like pickles and cupcakes, or tomatoes and ice cream.

Some good store-bought picnic food:
- Cheese and crackers
- Pudding or gelatin snack cups
- Beef jerky
- Dried fruit snacks
- Deli sandwiches
- Granola bars

PICNIC FUN

If getting to the picnic and enjoying your surprise food isn't enough, you could also play some games.

SIMON SAYS

Choose one person to be Simon. Everyone else stands in a line, facing Simon.

Simon gives a command, such as "raise your right hand," or "pull your left ear." Sometimes Simon says **"Simon Says"** before giving the command. If Simon says **"Simon Says,"** everyone else does what they are told.

If Simon does NOT say **"Simon Says,"** anyone who does what they are told is out of the game.

The last person left is the winner. They get to be the new Simon.

20 QUESTIONS

One person is chosen by the other players to think of something. The other players start asking questions that can be answered yes or no, and try to figure out what the leader is thinking of. For example:

◆ Is it a person?
◆ Is it a place?
◆ Is it a thing?
◆ Is it alive?
◆ Is it larger than your head?
◆ Can we see it from here?
◆ Is it red?

The first person to guess what the leader is thinking of becomes the new leader. They think of something new and the other players ask questions.

Plan plenty of time for your picnic. Rushed picnics aren't as fun as slow, lazy ones.

FOLLOW ME

Form a circle. Begin the game by having one player do an action, such as putting her thumbs to her ears and wiggling her fingers. The player beside her must repeat that action.

After performing the first action, the second player adds one of his own, such as sticking out his tongue. The next player after that must repeat, in order, all the actions of the other players up to that point and then add another.

Keep going around the circle until you can't remember any more actions. Then start over and try to think of totally new actions that weren't done before.

CRAZY CREATURES

What you need:

- paper
- pens or pencils for everyone

What do you get when you cross a family reunion with a picnic?
ANTS AND UNCLES.

What you do:

Each person takes a piece of paper and folds it into thirds, (like you would do if you were putting it into an envelope).

On the top third of the paper, draw a head of anything you want—rooster, Santa Claus, an alien, etc. Make sure you draw only the head on the top third of the paper. Don't tell anyone what you are drawing.

Draw neck lines from the head into the middle part of the paper (just over the fold), and fold the paper so that only the middle section shows. Switch papers with someone else. Don't peek!

Draw the middle part of someone, starting from the neck lines and only using the middle part of the paper. Draw any kind of body you like—try adding muscles, jewelry, or even multiple arms.

Draw leg lines from the body down into the top part of the last section (just over the fold). Fold the paper so that only the bottom section with the leg lines is showing.

Switch papers once again and draw legs, tentacles, or even claws from the leg lines.

When you are finished, unfold the papers and show each other your crazy creatures!

Beach Picnic

Why will you never go hungry at the beach? Because of the SAND WHICH IS there! Hot sun, hot fun, great food—there's nothing like a picnic at the beach!

PICNIC FOOD

- ◆ **Hot Dogs (if you have a fire pit)**
- ◆ Tuna Salad Sandwiches (if you don't)
- ◆ **Potato Chips**
- ◆ "Under the Sea" Finger Jell-O
- ◆ **S'more Sandwiches**

HOT DOGS

What you need:

- ◆ Hot dogs
- ◆ Hot dog buns
- ◆ Ketchup
- ◆ Mustard
- ◆ Coat hanger or stick

What you do:

1. Have an adult help you build a fire in the fire pit. When it has burned for awhile so the flames are low and you have coals, skewer your hot dog on a coat hanger or stick.

2. Hold the hot dog over the fire to cook it. Don't get it too close or it will get dirty with ashes. Keep turning it so it cooks evenly.

3. When it is done just how you like it, put it in a bun and add ketchup and mustard.

Makes 1 hot dog

TUNA SALAD SANDWICHES

What you need:

◆ I can tuna fish
◆ 2 tiny garlic dill pickles
◆ ¹/₄ cup mayonnaise
◆ salt and pepper
◆ 4 slices bread

What you do:

1. Open the tuna and squeeze all the extra liquid out of the can.

2. Cut the pickles into very small pieces.

3. Put the tuna, pickles, mayonnaise, and a few shakes of salt and pepper in a mixing bowl. Mix well.

4. Spread the tuna on 2 slices of bread and top with the remaining 2 slices of bread.

Makes 2 sandwiches

> What floats on the ocean and has a hundred eyes? POTATO SHIPS.

> Buy potato chips at the grocery store.

"Under the Sea" Finger Jell-O

What you need:

- 2 large boxes Berry Blue Jell-O or Lime Jell-O
- 2 1/2 cups boiling water

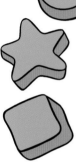

What you do:

1. Put Jell-O in a large glass 9 x 13-inch pan. Have an adult help you carefully prepare and pour in the boiling water.

2. Mix with a wooden spoon until the Jell-O dissolves.

3. Cover with plastic wrap or lid and put in the refrigerator until it sets (about 3 hours).

4. Cut in small squares and eat with your fingers. You can also use small cookie cutters to cut out different shapes.

Makes 24 servings

S'More Sandwiches

What you need:

- 2 chocolate chip cookies
- 1 large marshmallow
- Coat hanger or stick

What you do:

1. Have an adult help you build a fire in the fire pit. When the flames are low and you have coals, skewer your marshmallow on a coat hanger or stick.

2. Roast your marshmallow over the fire. Remember to keep turning it so it gets nice and brown all over.

3. When your marshmallow is done, slide it off the stick between 2 cookies.

Makes 1 cookie sandwich

PICNIC FUN

EGGS TO SEA

What you need:

- ◆ hard-boiled eggs
- ◆ markers
- ◆ sculpting tools, such as paper cups, plasticware, or driftwood

What you do:

Build a sandcastle near the waterline. Each person can build their own, or everyone can work together. Choose a place where there is plenty of wet sand and use your tools to make great designs.

Draw faces on the eggs and have them "people" your castle. Act out stories and adventures. If you are very daring, build your castle close to the water. See how much you can build before the waves knock it over. Have your egg people defend the castle against the incoming waves.

You don't just have to make a sandcastle—try a whole village, sand furniture, animals, or people.

BEACHCOMBING

What you need:

- a sack or bag, like a beach bag or a grocery sack
- a friend or two

What you do:

Walk slowly along the beach looking for anything interesting—shells, unusual bits of driftwood, different colors of sea glass, or floats from fishing nets. If you find something you like, put it in your sack.

Pay attention to clumps of seaweed, which sometimes hide treasures. Maybe you'll find shrimp or small crabs. Watch out for jellyfish—they sting!

If your beach has tidepools, look closely for fish and other sea creatures trapped inside these natural aquariums.

Low tide is the best time for beachcombing, because high tide waves push things up high on the beach, and low tide waves leave them exposed. Don't pick up anything that looks sharp or dangerous—or alive!

Don't wander too far from your picnic area. Make sure you always know where you are.

SHARKS AND SEALS

What you do:
Using a shovel, stick, or
your feet, make paths in the
sand in the shape of a giant
spoked wheel (like a ship's steering wheel). It
should have a hub in the center, with spokes going out to a rim.

Choose one player to be the Shark. The rest are seals.

The Shark tries to catch the seals. Everyone must stay on the paths. If a seal steps off the path, he is caught. Seals are safe in the hub, but only one seal at a time can be in the hub.

When a seal is caught, he becomes the Shark.

When is an ocean wave the most friendly?
AT HI TIDE.

FEED THE BIRDS

What you need:

◆ bread
◆ crackers

What you do:

Look for seabirds. Toss crackers or pieces of bread to the birds. See how close you can get the birds to come to you by throwing the food just in front of them and slowly putting it closer and closer to you.

You can also feed the birds in flight. As the birds fly overhead, throw the bread high. You'll be surprised at how good some birds are at catching their food in mid-air.

Take **extra water** for drinking, washing, and pouring on your head when it's too hot.

Drive-in Picnic

Sitting on the hood of the family car, eating delicious picnic food and waiting for the movie to begin—it's what families did for fun many years ago. Today, the joy of the drive-in theater picnic is slowly disappearing. But you can bring it back to life.

PICNIC FOOD

- Apple Slices and Caramel Dip
- **Veggies and Dip**
- String Cheese and Crackers
- **Popcorn or Boxed Caramel Corn**
- Chips and Salsa
- **Peanut Butter Cookies**

APPLE SLICES AND CARAMEL DIP

What you need:

- ◆ 1 package (14 ounces) caramel candies
- ◆ 2 teaspoons water
- ◆ 2 to 4 apples

What you do:

1. Unwrap caramel candies and put them in a medium saucepan. Add the water.

2. Cook over medium heat, stirring constantly, until caramels melt. Cool slightly.

3. Pour into a serving bowl.

4. Cut the apples in quarters and remove the cores. Then cut into slices. Serve with caramel dip.

Makes 4 to 8 servings

VEGGIES AND DIP

What you need:

- ◆ 1 carton (8 ounces) sour cream
- ◆ 1 package ranch dressing mix
- ◆ 1 red bell pepper
- ◆ 1 cucumber
- ◆ 1 bag baby carrots
- ◆ 1 can olives

What you do:

1. Put the sour cream in a bowl and add the ranch dressing mix. Stir together until it is combined. Keep it covered in the refrigerator while you prepare the vegetables.

2. Wash the bell pepper. Cut out the stem and then cut it in half. Remove the seeds and clean it out. Cut it into thin slices.

3. Wash and peel the cucumber. Cut off the ends, and then cut it in thin slices.

4. Put the carrots in a serving bowl. Open the olives, drain the liquid, and put the olives in a serving bowl.

5. Serve the veggies with dip.

> Buy string cheese, crackers, popcorn or boxed caramel corn, and chips at the grocery store.

FRESH SALSA

What you need:

- 4 roma tomatoes
- 1/4 cup chopped fresh cilantro
- 1/2 small white or red onion
- juice of 1 lime
- salt and pepper
- corn chips

What you do:

1. Wash the tomatoes and remove the stem area. Dice into small pieces.

2. Chop the cilantro.

3. Cut the onion in half and remove the outer skin. Dice half into small pieces.

4. Mix all the chopped ingredients together in a large bowl. Add the lime juice and several shakes of salt and pepper. Serve with corn chips.

Makes 6 to 8 servings

PEANUT BUTTER COOKIES

What you need:

- ◆ 1 cup sugar
- ◆ 1 cup creamy peanut butter
- ◆ 1 egg
- ◆ 18 to 20 Hershey's chocolate kisses, unwrapped

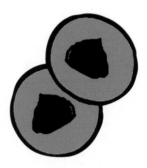

What you do:

1. Mix the sugar, peanut butter, and egg together in a bowl.

2. Take a piece of dough in your hands and roll it into a 1-inch ball. Keep doing this until you have made all the dough into balls. Place evenly apart on a cookie sheet.

3. Press your thumb in the center of each cookie to make an indent. Set a chocolate kiss into the indent in the center of each one.

4. Bake at 350 degrees for 12 minutes. Using hot pads, take the cookie sheet out of the oven and put cookies on a rack to cool.

Makes 18 to 20 cookies

Why did the cookie go to the doctor? Because it was feeling crummy!

PICNIC FUN

Ask a grown-up to help you set up your drive-in theater. The screen can be your living room TV, a TV carried out to the lawn, or an in-car DVD. Seats can be couches, blankets, or the seats in your car. The movie? Your choice!

If you are lucky enough to live near an actual, real drive-in theater, pack up your picnic and have Mom and Dad take you. It's an experience you'll never forget.

Go ahead and put on your pajamas, wait until sunset, turn off the lights, and eat while you watch the movie.

MOVIE GAMES

BEFORE THE MOVIE

Silent Movie—One person is chosen to silently act out a movie of their choice. Other players try to guess the name of the movie. The player who guesses correctly gets to act out the next silent movie.

DURING THE PREVIEWS AND CREDITS

The Alphabet Game—As you wait for the movie to begin, see how many letters of the alphabet you can find on the screen. Go in order, from A to Z. Work together and shout out the letter when you see it.

DURING THE MOVIE

Do As They Do—Before the movie begins, decide on an action that you will all perform when you see something on the screen. For example:

- When you see someone run, everyone stand up and run in place.

- When you see an animal, make its sound. Bark when you see a dog. Chirp when you see a bird.

- Whenever you see a car, shout, "HONK HONK!"

- Whenever you hear the word "love," make loud kissy noises.

- Whenever you see a bad guy, shout, "Look Out!"

You can decide to do more funny actions on your own.

Movie Quiz—One person starts as the Quizmaster. The Quizmaster has the remote control. Begin watching the movie. At a place of the Quizmaster's choosing, he or she pauses the movie and asks a question about what you have just seen. For example:

- What color was the dog?

- What was the last word the main character said?

- Did the main character just eat apples or oranges?

- How many times did the doorbell ring in that scene?

The first person to get the answer right gets to be the next Quizmaster.

What was the pirate movie rated?
ARRR!

Create Your Own Picnic

Now you have the idea, there are a million and one ways to have a picnic. By following these four simple steps, you can have more fun than any kid should be allowed to have.

 ## STEP 1: PICK A PLACE

- amusement park
- back of a truck
- barn
- baseball diamond
- boat
- bowling alley
- bridge
- campground
- car
- classroom
- closet
- elevator
- garden

- gazebo
- ghost town
- golf course
- Grandma's house
- gym
- playground

- swimming pool
- tennis court
- tent
- train
- tree house
- waterfall
- zoo

STEP 2: CHOOSE YOUR FOOD

- burritos
- bread and cheese
- cake
- candy bars
- cereal
- cheese and crackers
- chips
- deli food
- fast food

- fried chicken
- fruits
- hamburgers
- hot dogs
- leftovers
- nuts and raisins
- pie
- pizza
- salad

- sandwiches
- vegetables

STEP 3: SELECT ACTIVITIES

- backpacking
- baseball
- basketball
- board games
- boating
- capture the flag
- charades
- checkers
- chess
- croquet
- drawing
- dominoes
- fishing
- football
- Frisbee
- hide and seek

- hiking
- hopscotch
- jumping rope
- keep away
- kite flying
- leapfrog
- marbles
- obstacle race
- puzzles
- reading
- skateboarding
- skating
- soccer
- swimming
- tag
- tic-tac-toe

- tug-of-war
- tumbling
- volleyball

STEP 4: HAVE FUN!

Leave your picnic spot **cleaner** than you found it. Pick up garbage others have left.